IN MY BACKYARD

chipmunks

by Lindsy J. O'Brien

CREATIVE EDUCATION • CREATIVE PAPERBACKS

Published by Creative Education and Creative Paperbacks
P.O. Box 227, Mankato, Minnesota 56002
Creative Education and Creative Paperbacks are imprints of
The Creative Company
www.thecreativecompany.us

Design and production by Chelsey Luther
Art direction by Rita Marshall
Printed in China

Photographs by Corbis (Gary Carter, ASO FUJITA/
amanaimagesRF/amanaimages), Dreamstime (Isselee, Brian
Lasenby, Charles McCarthy, Stephan Pietzko, Sandra Van
Der Steen), Getty Images (Frank Cezus, Takao Onozato/
Aflo, Leonard Lee Rue III), Science Source (Tom McHugh),
Shutterstock (allanw, Michael C. Gray, Eric Isselee, stock_shot,
unpict)

Library of Congress Cataloging-in-Publication Data
O'Brien, Lindsy J.
Chipmunks / by Lindsy J. O'Brien.
p. cm. — (In my backyard)
Includes bibliographical references and index.
Summary: A high-interest introduction to the life cycle of
chipmunks, including how pups develop, their plant-based
diet, threats from predators, and the burrowed habitats of
these backyard animals.

ISBN 978-1-60818-697-6 (hardcover)
ISBN 978-1-62832-293-4 (pbk)
ISBN 978-1-56660-733-9 (eBook)
1. Chipmunks—Juvenile literature.

QL737.R68 O34 2016
599.36/4—dc23   2015034582

CCSS: RI.1.1, 2, 3, 4, 5, 6, 7; RI.2.1, 2, 4, 5, 6, 7, 10; RF.1.1, 3, 4;
RF.2.3, 4

First Edition HC 9 8 7 6 5 4 3 2 1
First Edition PBK 9 8 7 6 5 4 3 2 1

Contents

You hear a sound in the bushes. Out pops a furry, striped head. The head is so small it could fit in your hand. Two puffy cheeks tell you this is a chipmunk.

mushrooms

Chipmunks' cheeks puff out as they eat mushrooms and other foods.

Baby chipmunks are called pups. Newborn pups are pink and hairless. Three to five pups are born in one litter. Pups leave their litters after only eight weeks.

A chipmunk that has babies in summer may have another litter in late fall.

There are about 25 chipmunk species. Most chipmunks are red or brown. They have brown stripes on their backs and faces. That is one way to tell chipmunks apart from striped squirrels.

chipmunk

squirrel

Chipmunks have 5 toes on each front foot and 4 toes on the back—opposite of squirrels.

Chipmunks like places where there are trees or bushes. They dig **burrows** under the ground. The burrows can be as long as 10 feet (3 m)!

Chipmunks use their front feet and cheek pouches to move dirt for burrows.

Do you like to eat fungi? Chipmunks do! They also gather seeds and nuts. They move their food from place to place. This spreads seeds and fungi around the forest. New plants grow.

A chipmunk can sleep 15 hours a day! A sleeping chipmunk can hide from predators. Owls, foxes, cats, and people hunt chipmunks.

In winter, chipmunks sleep for weeks and wake up to eat stored food.

When it is not sleeping, the chipmunk looks for food. It makes a "chip-chip-chip" sound as it searches. Chipmunks were named after that sound.

Chipmunks move their paws and make birdlike chirping sounds, too.

17

Chipmunks are helpful in the forest. But they can make problems for people. Keep your eyes and ears open. You might find a chipmunk stealing birdseed in your backyard!

Chipmunks often steal food from birdfeeders in home gardens.

Chipmunks dig burrows. Burrows have all kinds of rooms. The cache (or larder) is used to store food. Chipmunks build a place to sleep, too. A trash tunnel is made for garbage. Chipmunk "garbage" is made of droppings, shells from nuts, and other items.

Materials you need: pencil, crayons or markers, and paper

Make a Burrow

1. Starting with the main tunnel, draw a chipmunk burrow. Be sure there is an entrance and an exit!

2. Draw tunnels and rooms off the main room. Start with the cache, the sleeping area, and the trash room. Where should the trash room go? Next to the bedroom? Probably not! What would make life easiest for a chipmunk?

3. Now be creative. What other types of rooms does a chipmunk need? Draw these, too.

If you have more time, draw a line at the top of your paper. Above that, draw objects that might be above the ground near a burrow. Where would a chipmunk choose to build its burrow?

ENTER

cache

treasure

Glossary

burrows: holes or tunnels dug in the ground

fungi: non-animal life forms that grow like plants; a fungus feeds off dead animals or plants

litter: a group of animal babies born at the same time

predators: animals that hunt other animals for food

species: groups of living things that are closely related

Read More

Gregory, Josh. *Chipmunks*.
New York: Children's Press, 2015.

Sebastian, Emily. *Chipmunks*.
New York: PowerKids Press, 2012.

Websites

National Geographic Kids: Chipmunk
http://kids.nationalgeographic.com/animals/chipmunk/
Find out more about chipmunks, and watch a Zooville video!

National Wildlife Federation: Chipmunk Game
http://www.nwf.org/Kids/Games/Chipmunks-Game.aspx
Follow the directions to play a game about chipmunks.

Note: Every effort has been made to ensure that the websites listed above are suitable for children, that they have educational value, and that they contain no inappropriate material. However, because of the nature of the Internet, it is impossible to guarantee that these sites will remain active indefinitely or that their contents will not be altered.

Index